LURIE'S ALMANAC

LURIE'S ALMANAC

by Ranan Lurie

Andrews and McMeel, Inc.
A Universal Press Syndicate Company
Kansas City • New York

Much of this material was published in England 1982 by Martin Secker & Warburg Limited.

ISBN: 0-8362-1252-5 (hard) 0-8362-1253-3 (paper)

Library of Congress Catalog Card Number: 83-70266

To Daphne

Introduction

When Ranan Lurie came to us at *The Times* to start as a guest resident cartoonist he told us that every cartoon was like a four-wheel vehicle. The wheels were the humour, the drawing of the metaphor, the caricature and the facts. The vehicle itself was the message the cartoon had to convey to the reader. I remember feeling somewhat startled at his arrival, because *The Times* had not been accustomed to the presence of a resident cartoonist and certainly not one who appeared to have such a precise and perfectionist idea of his role. Moreover, there appeared to be a danger that Lurie had expectations at *The Times* which we would not be able to fulfil, unused as we were to the medium which he so ably projected.

My fears were unfounded as it turned out. Although he had not inhabited the culture of a British newspaper before he quickly fitted in with the homely routine of a newspaper office, which is in such contrast with the dramatic events it seeks to distil and publish every day. He attended our daily editorial conferences, made shrewd contributions from the back of the room, with a courtesy and insight borne of his wide international experience. We were, after all, host not to a caricaturist who had political aspirations, but to a man who was at heart a political analyst who believed that his analysis could most often be most appropriately projected in the form of a cartoon.

Lurie is a sixth-generation Israeli. He grew up in Israel and has served as a parachute major in the Israeli Army. He occupied numerous positions on Israeli papers before emigrating to the United States and becoming a naturalised American in 1974. From then on his political horizons widened exponentially. His cartoons became syndicated all over the Western world and he won many awards.

It was thus a privilege for us at *The Times* to become the launching pad for Lurie's syndicated cartoons. I believe that a cartoonist, like the best columnists, should always have a point of view which is not necessarily synchronised with the editorial policy of the parent body; indeed, a state of tension existing between the cartoonist and the newspaper adds considerably to the interest value. One only has to remember Vicky publishing his cartoons in the Beaverbrook newspapers to savour the creative effect of this tension. That has often been the case between *The Times* and Lurie's cartoons, and all the more welcome for that.

Fortunately his gifts as a caricaturist have also not gone unnoticed in *The Times*, where many of our profiles have been dramatically enhanced by the advantage of a very distinctive Lurie caricature.

His work appears in 45 countries and is published in 400 newspapers with a combined circulation of 62 million. Not surprisingly, therefore, his sojourn on *The Times* has been a temporary one since a man with that kind of international personality is not likely to be pinned down for long. There is a restlessness about his quest for perfection which suggests to me that he will never be fully satisfied in any permanent context. The world is his oyster and is likely to give forth his pearls for a long time to come.

Charles Douglas-Home
Editor
The Times

Ronald Reagan,
Presidential Candidate

Carter

1980

The year was dominated by two events, one sporting, one political. The major political event was the Olympic Games. In sport, the American presidential election held the headlines. Russia invaded Afghanistan, America retaliated by ordering its athletes not to invade Russia. The American hostages spent most of the year in custody in Iran, and Jimmy Carter lost face, several servicemen, a helicopter or two, much time and the election failing to get them out. In Poland, the People's Democracy spent ineffectual energy wondering what to do about the People, who busied themselves forming a trade union and indulging in odd democratic excesses like going on strike. This was thought by the other Warsaw Pact countries to be undesirable, and there was much speculation as to whether the Russians might come gently to the aid of the People in the traditional way: with troops, tanks and guns. The Middle East simmered, Japan's economy grew stronger, the arms race gained pace—but then what's new?

MOSCOW
AFGHANISTAN
FRANCE
BELGIUM
IRELAND
ICELAND
ITALY
SWEDEN
LURIE

TROOP WITHDRAWAL
AFGHANISTAN
LURIE

NOVEMBER
Unemployment
Inflation
LURIE©

'Well done. Now execute each other'

'Boy, are we lucky it was only a limited nuclear war!'

'Tora! Tora! Tora!'

POLAND
GIEREK
HUNGER
LURIE
SUNDAY TIMES, LONDON

SOVIET ECONOMIC AID
Poland
LURIE

WORLD'S OIL SUPPLY
WORLD'S OIL SUPPLY
Iran
Iraq
LURIE ©
SUNDAY TIMES, LONDON

'Jump!'

'OK—Who's first?'

Colonel Quaddafi of Libya: the new Afro look

January–March, 1981

Some fuses lit in 1980 burned on nicely. Iran handed the American hostages to Ronald Reagan as an inauguration present. The Ayatollah was now pre-occupied with holding off an unexpected Iraqi invasion. Planes, guns and tanks, bought on an instalment plan by the Shah from the Great Satan, turned out to work equally well on behalf of the Khomeini troops. As each air force seemed content to do little but blow up the other side's oil refineries, there was some quiet speculation as to whether the world might shortly run out of oil. Invasion being all the rage, Libya's Colonel Quaddafi was caught red-handed invading Chad. In the West, the world watched Mrs Thatcher's great economic experiment with fascination. Unemployment was clearly a growth industry under monetarism, as was inflation. Could Ronald Reagan do the same for America?

'D'ya mind closin' up when you're done?'

I.
HOSTAGES

II.
$
LURIE ©

QADDAFI
CHAD
LURIE

Jose Napoleon Duarte, President of El Salvador

April–June, 1981

Will they, won't they? The Russians hovered over Poland threatening invasion. Not wishing to be left out, Ronald Reagan hovered over El Salvador offering military aid and 'advisers' to the Junta, who were at the time engaged in a noisy war with their own peasants. To everyone's astonishment, OPEC was forced to confess that there was an oil glut, and prices fell. Further astonishment was provided by Ronald Reagan showing signs of carrying out his campaign pledges to cut back government intervention in the economy and help business. A politician doing what he promised? What was the world coming to?

POLAND

AFGHANISTAN will be their VIET NAM!
EL SALVADOR will be their AFGHANISTAN!
the MIDDLE EAST will be their EL SALVADOR!

SMALL
BIZ
BIG BIZ
LURIE

'Our oil glut starts to worry me, sir'

'On your marks . . . get set . . .'

François Mitterand

July, 1981

Suddenly everybody seemed to be talking about money. Where had it all gone? Could we have some back, please? The heads of government of the seven great industrial nations met in Ottawa and tried to borrow some from each other. Unemployment rose, so did prices. So did M. Mitterand, French Socialist leader and everybody's unexpected favourite for turning out to be a hawk when it came to dealing with the Russians. A few token Communists in the French cabinet could make sure the trains ran on time, leaving it to M. Mitterand to make sure France's H-bombs and thriving arms export industry were equally punctual. In Britain, a Royal wedding took everyone's mind off gloom and despair.

'Damned Communists!'

Ottawa summit, a friendly handshake

1.
Welcome to the Ottawa Summit
INTEREST RATES
LURIE
THE TIMES, LONDON

2.
INTEREST RATES

MY
WAY
PARTY
LOYALISTS
LURIE ©
THE TIMES, LONDON

LURIE
THE TIMES, LONDON

Castro

August, 1981

The traditional silly season failed to live up to its name for most of the world. In Poland the rumblings from Moscow grew louder and more menacing. America pondered out loud that perhaps a neutron bomb might be a good idea after all. The sentiment was not much shared by Russia, or, for that matter, West Germany, where the prospect of a bomb that killed people while leaving the buildings unblemished sounded good if you were a washing-machine but less attractive if you were a German. South Africa sent troops into Angola, where they fought with Cubans, demonstrating that in today's army you can enjoy exotic travel while meeting interesting and varied new natives. In the Middle East, President Sadat and Premier Begin undertook to solve the problem of the Palestinians without actually bothering the Palestinians with the details. Meanwhile, the Palestinians took to shooting impartially in all directions. This came to be known as the Peace Process.

THE FUTURE
Poland
LURIE
THE TIMES, LONDON

'After all, we're all in the same boat'

'He-l-l-l-p!'

‘OK—we’ll count to three, and start moving it’

SOUTH AFRICA
ANGOLA
LURIE
THE TIMES, LONDON

Mr President

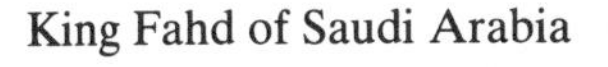
King Fahd of Saudi Arabia

September, 1981

It was hard to know where to go to be safe. Not Iran, where the Islamic Revolution continued to reform the local population by eliminating it with tireless enthusiasm. Not Poland, where a panicky government took to locking up free trade unionists. Not even America, where Reaganomics turned out to mean more for the little guy—if what the little guy wanted was more unemployment, higher interest rates, more welfare cuts and the privilege of paying for bigger and better missiles. President Reagan undertook to make Saudi Arabia safe by supplying them with AWACS early warning aircraft, although there was some dispute over who they would be safe against. Us? said the Israelis. Not so, said the President. Then who? said the Israelis. High flying Ayatollahs, said the Americans, with an eye to the Islamic Revolution threatening to spread from the North. Or even oil-thirsty Russian soldiers bored with spending their winters in Afghanistan.

'Now that you've learned your lesson, let's continue with the revolution!'

NEW ARMS RACE
ARMS
CE
LURIE
THE TIMES, LONDON

'There's an AWACS in my soup!'

'We'd better isolate him'

'And twenty years ago all this was desert'

LURIE THE TIMES, LONDON
POLAND

'Looks like poor planning, Mr President'

President Sadat of Egypt

October, 1981

Muslim fanatics assassinated Anwar Sadat of Egypt, and suddenly the world seemed an even more dangerous place than usual. Any doubt as to whether Sadat was a good guy vanished as the international league of bad guys expressed varying degrees of pleasure at his departure. If Quaddafi of Libya and Khomeini of Iran were both pleased that he was dead, the rest of the world knew what to think. It provided an unwelcome distraction from economic problems, which seemed to grow worse each day. Now that the world's economic casualty section had a new team of healers—led by Nurse Thatcher and Ambulance-driver Reagan—muffled cries of pain from the patient seemed to suggest the healthy leg had been amputated by mistake.

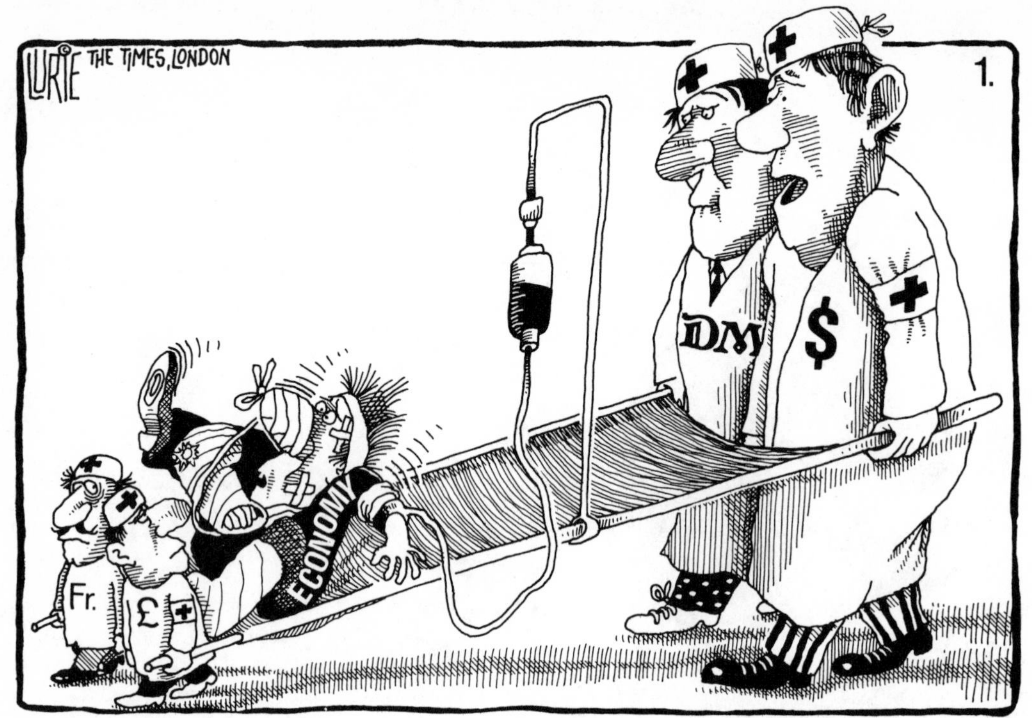

'The poor patient is suffering—let's realign!'

MX
TAX PAYER
LURIE©
THE TIMES, LONDON

'We *want* to follow in his footsteps—but where are they?'

MIDEAST
SADAT
LURIE
THE TIMES, LONDON

LURIE

FREE-WORLD
ECONOMISTS
LURIE
THE TIMES, LONDON

EEC
NATO
ITALY
BENELUX
FRANCE
U.K.
GREECE
GERMANY
U.S.
CANADA
LURIE
THE TIMES, LONDON

NORTH
SOUTH
LURIE
THE TIMES, LONDON

I
R
A
LURIE
THE TIMES, LONDON

USSR
SOVIET ECONOMY
AFGHANISTAN
ARMS RACE
POLAND
LURIE ©
THE TIMES, LONDON

'See how I'm holding the whole damn Middle East together?'

REAGANOMICS
LURIE ©
THE TIMES, LONDON

Begin

Zenko Suzuki, Japan's Premier

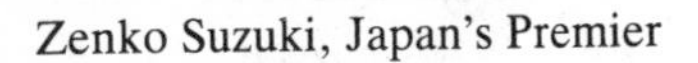

December, 1981

Peace and goodwill appeared to have been cancelled. Disarmament talks bogged down in a swamp of initials. How many MIRV-ed MXs made an SS-20? Nobody seemed to have the details. Israeli Premier Begin's contribution to goodwill among men was a series of personal attacks on world leaders. Only an Eskimo mayor or two were spared. The Japanese Prime Minister sacked most of his cabinet. The Polish Communist party asserted its role as the true voice of the silent toiling masses by locking up any member of the aforementioned masses who wasn't silent or wasn't toiling. This seemed to include most of the population. Europe suffered one of its harshest winters, in keeping with the general spirit of the times.

Disarmament
Disarmament
LURIE
THE TIMES, LONDON

Nowhere to move

Suzuki
JAPAN'S CABINET
LURIE
THE TIMES, LONDON

SOLIDARITY
POLISH COMMUNIST PARTY
LURIE
THE TIMES, LONDON

AFGHANISTAN
POLAND
©
LURIE
THE TIMES,
LONDON

'You-no-good-Carrington!..'
'You rotten Schmidt!..'
'You ugly EEC, filthy UN!..'
'You, antisemitic USA!..'
'You, treacherous Israeli opposition!..'
'See? didn't I tell you?
the world hates us!'
LURIE THE TIMES, LONDON

French extention
German-Soviet gas pipeline
LURIE
THE TIMES, LONDON

Leonid Brezhnev

Lech Walesa, Polish Trade Union Leader

January, 1982

Relaxation was the word on everybody's lips. Poland relaxed some of its emergency laws, rather like a tank-driver changing from top gear to second before running over somebody. In the spirit of further relaxation, all restrictions on Jew-baiting were removed, and anti-Semites were at last given an opportunity to describe the damage Polish Jews were causing to Poland. The fact that there are no Jews left in Poland was accepted by the population as merely another inconvenient shortage, along with those of bread and salami.

'See? Didn't I promise to let you out once you behave?'

Warsaw Pact winter exercises begin

'Ouch . . . these Jews are still everywhere!'

Helmut Schmidt, Ex-Chancellor of West Germany

February, 1982

Suddenly everybody seemed to need rescuing. Ronald Reagan offered again to rescue El Salvador, an offer which a number of El Salvadoreans politely declined. Everything to do with trains needed rescuing: Sir Freddie Laker's cheap air fares on SkyTrain looked like sinking with the rest of his airline. Mrs Thatcher said she didn't think she should bale him out. British Rail ground to a halt, and had to be rescued by an inquiry. Finally, various governments shyly admitted that they were hard at work on new biological, chemical and neutron weapons and the world was left to wonder whether there would be anyone left to rescue. Germany wondered more passionately than most.

USA
EL SALVADOR
LURIE
THE TIMES, LONDON

LURIE ©
THE TIMES, LONDON
Latin America

LURIE ©
THE TIMES, LONDON
STRIKE
RAIL STRIKE
STRIKE!

HIGHER AIR FARE PRICES
LAKER
LURIE ©
THE TIMES, LONDON

CONVENTIO
WAR
2
NERVE
GAS
NUCLEAR
WARFARE
BIOLOGICAL
WARFARE
LURIE THE TIMES, LONDON

Nkomo

Robert Mugabe of Zimbabwe

March, 1982

Nobody needed enemies: everybody seemed to be waging war on themselves. Reaganomics began to take effect in America and the government showed that its heart was with the little man by turning big businesses into small businesses. In Poland, the new military government spared the Russians the trouble of sending in tanks from the outside by doing the job for them. In Zimbabwe, Robert Mugabe sacked his old guerrilla-warfare partner Joshua Nkomo, and unemployed guerrillas relished the prospect of business as usual in a new and improved civil war. Only El Salvador saw its problems in terms of outside agitators; in this case the blame went to the United States 'advisers' sent there to help out.

'Poor grain? Nonsense—it's our best year ever!'

'Hold it . . . Comrade Brezhnev will be happy to deny personally the rumours about his death!'

U.S.
EL SALVADOR
JUNTA
LURIE ©
THE TIMES, LONDON

'I command you not to rise!'

'But I'm the astronaut it was supposed to take . . . remember?'

Pierre Trudeau,
Prime Minister of Canada

Ex-President L. Galtieri of Argentina

April, 1982

Everybody seemed to want to say goodbye to somebody. Quebec wanted to say goodbye to the rest of Canada. General Galtieri said goodbye noisily to 43 British marines and assorted Falkland Islanders as a preliminary to saying goodbye to his own career. At the disarmament talks the world said goodbye to sanity as both sides continued to squabble over who had most rockets pointed at whom. President Reagan declared modestly that what the world needed was more Reaganomics and to say goodbye to full employment.

'We're all in the same boat'

Tough decisions ahead

ARGENTINIAN
TAX PAYER
BRITISH
TAX PAYER
LURIE ©
THE TIMES, LONDON

Galtieri
S.D.P.
LABOUR
FALKLANDS
PUTSCH
LURIE
THE TIMES, LONDON

'It's OK, as long as we can see eye to eye'

'We want to separate and proceed independently'

'They must be scared to death by now'

Francis Pym, Foreign Secretary

Alexander Haig, former Secretary of State

May, 1982

Whose rock was it anyway? General Galtieri seemed to think that possession was nine-tenths of Argentinian law, that he was sitting on it and was not about to be shifted. Mrs Thatcher, who saw things the same way but from a British point of view, said that the General should jolly well go. Al Haig did not much know or care whose rock it was as long as it was British and people stopped jumping on and off it all the time, clutching bombs. Not that the General and Mrs Thatcher had a monopoly on bomb-fever. The war between Iran and Iraq livened up, Iran snatched back its lost territory and, like a driver whose brakes have failed, rolled on towards Baghdad. In Poland, the process of relaxation continued. Tank-drivers now removed their caps respectfully before running over members of the local populace.

big
tax
cuts
BIG
DEFENCE
SPENDING
LURIE ©
THE TIMES, LONDON

'Congratulations. We've decided to take the pressure off'

Haig's career
BBC
NBC
LURIE
THE TIMES, LONDON

Tip of the iceberg

'See? We're even watering it!'

USE BRITISH
made in Israel
BUY
FRENCH
Think American
Get American
trust West German goods
LURIE
THE TIMES, LONDON

'Looks as though they're taking off'

'Okay—you're all under arrest!'

'Ouch!'

LURIE ©
THE TIMES, LONDON
Iraq
GULF STATES

'As you can see, talks about a successor are premature'

Arafat

P. Habib,
US Special Ambassador

June, 1982

The Falkland Islands returned to Britain, and an impressive number of Argentinian prisoners returned to Argentina. Mrs Thatcher promised an inquiry into events leading up to the war. Exactly which events was the problem. Let us just look at the last few months when you made a mess of the whole thing. No, said Mrs Thatcher, let us look at the last 20 years so we can get a few of your mistakes in as well. Nobody except the Argentinians suggested going back 150 years. Meanwhile, the Israeli ambassador was shot by terrorists in London and Israel's premier Begin undertook to find the villains in Beirut. The search seemed to involve 60,000 troops scouring the ground in Lebanon and remodelling the towns that got in the way.

Spain joins NATO

'You're trying to tell me that now I'll have to leave all this?'

MIDDLE EAST
Terror
LURIE
THE TIMES, LONDON

'Okay, guys - duck and prepare for the world's reaction..!'
SOVIET WARNINGS
ARAB THREATS
U.N. MOVES
E.E.C. CONDEMNATION
LURIE
THE TIMES, LONDON

BEST RUNNER FOR 1982
PLO
ARGENTINA
IRAQ
SURRENDER
LURIE
THE TIMES, LONDON

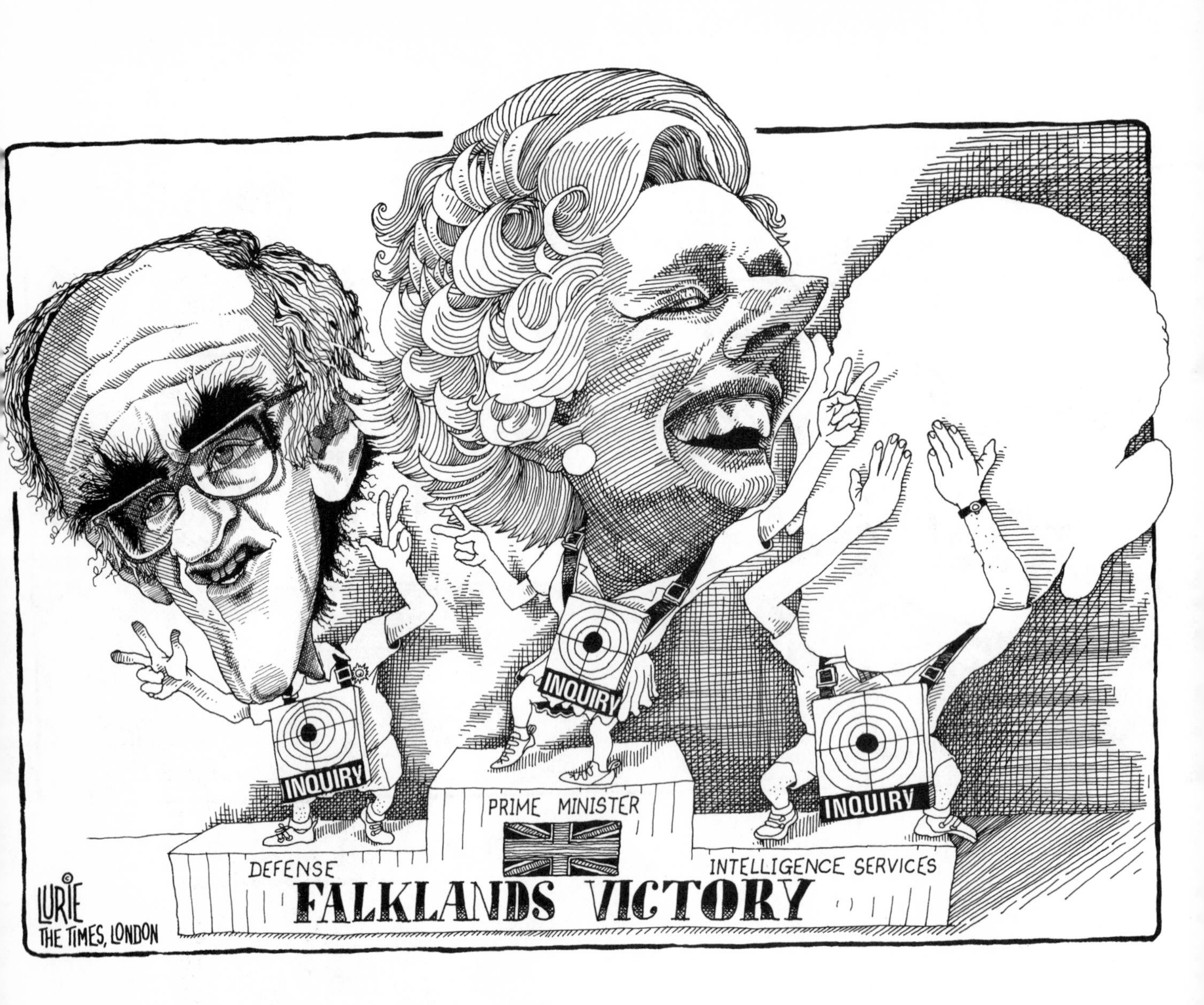
INQUIRY
INQUIRY
INQUIRY
PRIME MINISTER
DEFENSE
INTELLIGENCE SERVICES
FALKLANDS VICTORY
LURIE©
THE TIMES, LONDON

SYRIA
P.L.O.

SYRIA
P.L.O.
LURIE THE TIMES, LONDON

LEBANON
SOUTH ATLANTIC
LATIN AMERICA
AFGHANISTAN
POLAND
IRAN
LURIE©

World Cup '82

'Can anyone hear me?'

The Queen

George P. Shultz, Secretary of State

July, 1982

Impotence rules, okay? In Beirut, the Israelis failed to remove the PLO, the Russians failed to back the PLO, the Arab States failed to help the PLO, the Americans failed to negotiate with the PLO, and the long-suffering Lebanese failed to survive the presence of the PLO. In London the combined might of Scotland Yard and the Queen's 13 corgis failed to prevent a Mr Fagan from paying an unorthodox visit to Buckingham Palace, where he spent some time in early-morning conversation with Her Majesty in her bedroom. America's new Secretary of State, George Shultz, discovered that if diplomacy was the art of saying nice doggie while picking up a rock, the local Dobermen seemed to bite first and negotiate later. Even the almighty OPEC found that you could blackmail all of the world some of the time, but not all of the time. If oil supply outstripped demand, blackmailers' logic meant that prices fell.

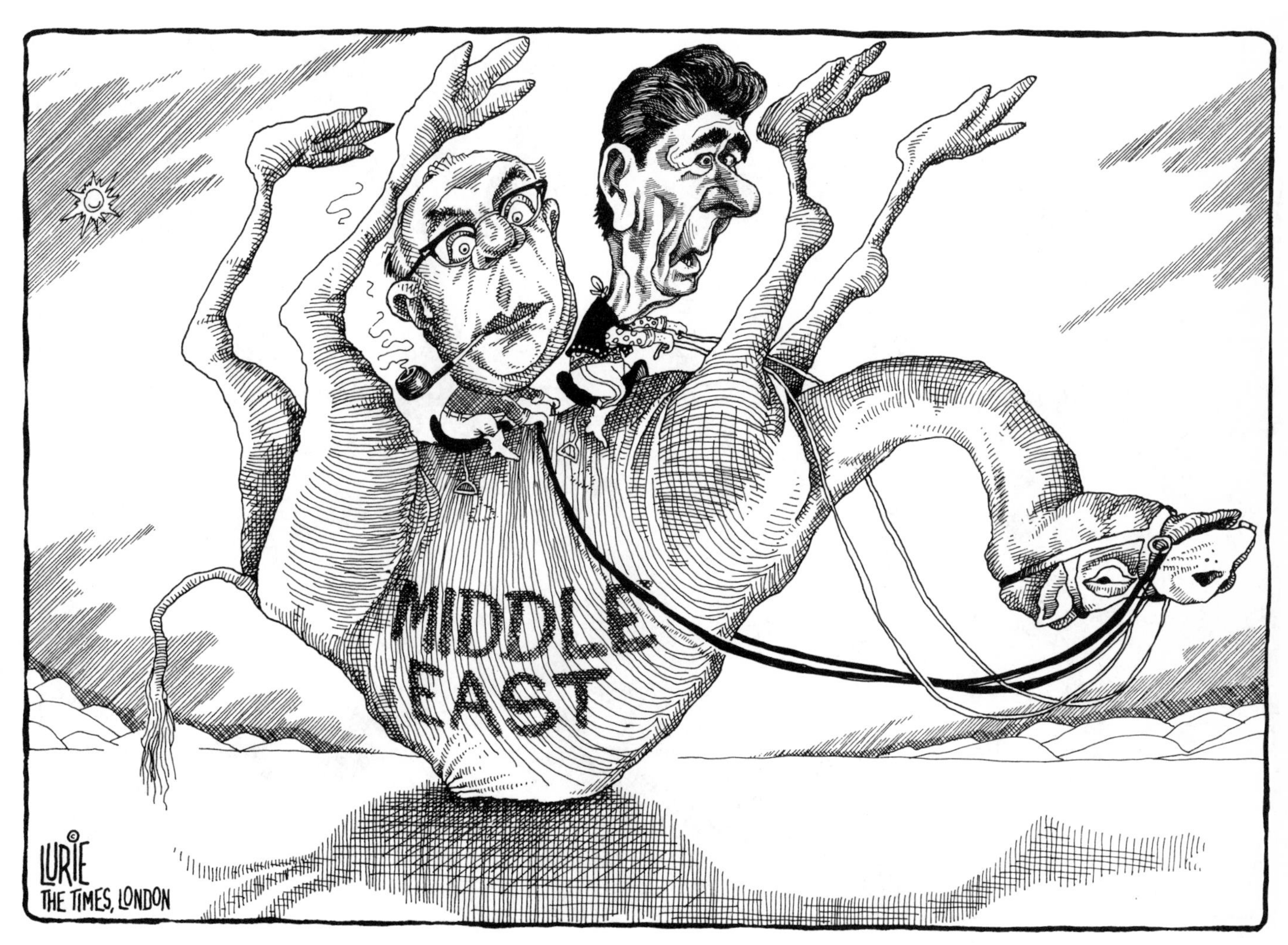

'Well, Shultz—you'll find it's not an easy animal to ride'

ARGENTINA
U.K.
LURIE ©
THE TIMES, LONDON

P.L.O.
BEIRUT
LURIE ©
THE TIMES
LONDON

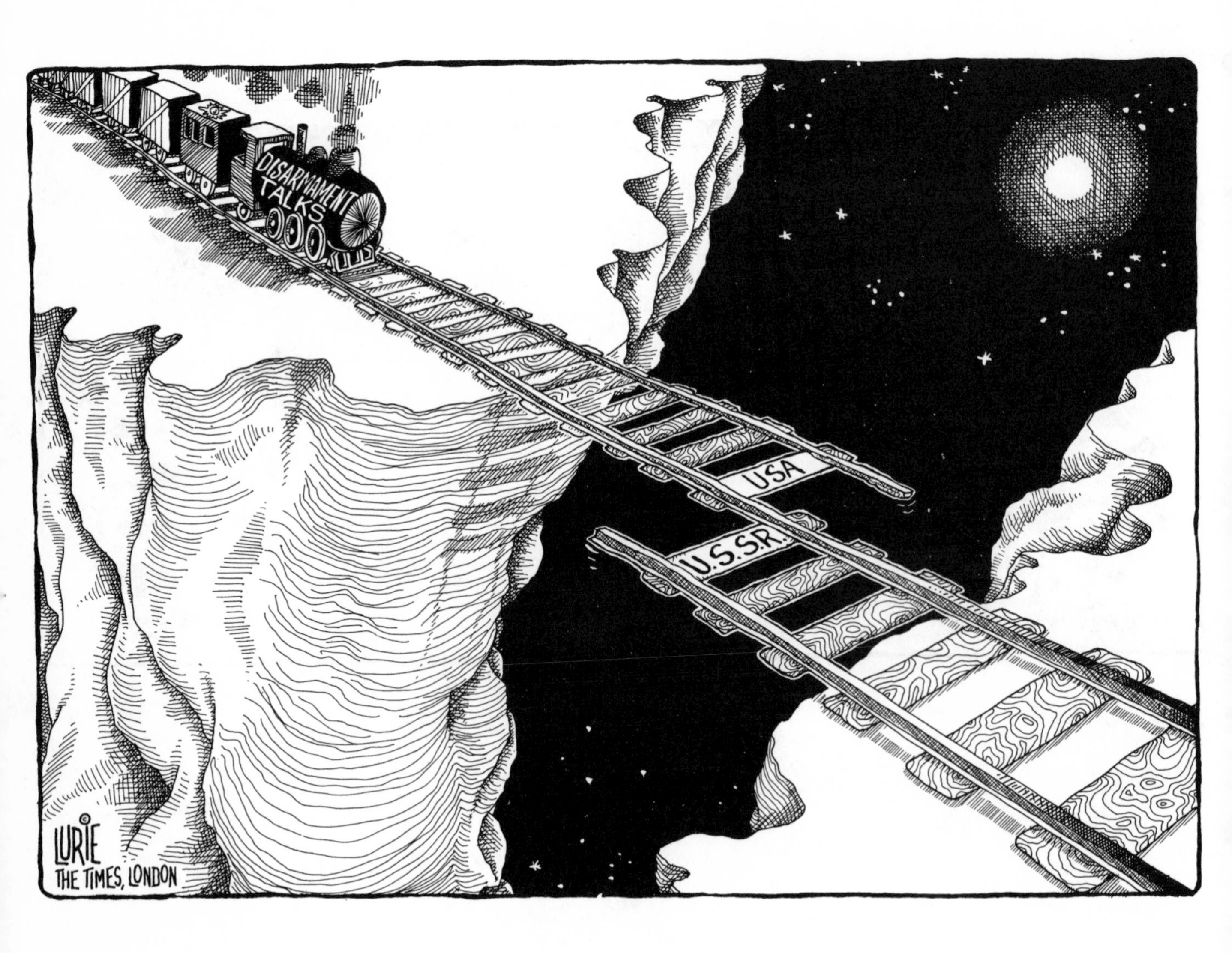
DISARMAMENT TALKS
USA
U.S.S.R.
LURIE
THE TIMES, LONDON

ARAB SOLIDARITY
SOVIET RELIABILITY
LEBANON
LURIE
THE TIMES, LONDON

Labour
Alliance
CONSERVATIVES
FALKLANDS INQUIRY
LURIE ©
THE TIMES, LONDON

INTEREST RATES
LURIE
THE TIMES, LONDON

LEBANON
LURIE
THE TIMES, LONDON

PRICE CUTS
PRICE CUTS
OPEC
OPEC
LURIE
THE TIMES, LONDON

'I've changed my mind—now I want it well-done!'

SHULTZ
© LURIE
THE TIMES, LONDON

SHULTZ
PRO
ISRA
LOB
LURIE ©
THE TIMES, LONDON

SCANDALS
'Best tourist season ever!'
LURIE
THE TIMES, LONDON

'And the winner is . . .'

THE PIPELINE
energy
gas
EEC
CASH
THE TIMES, LONDON

Colonel Quaddafi

Egyptian President Hosni Mubarak

John Paul II

Assad

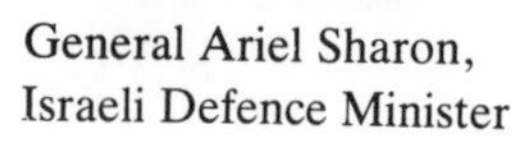

General Ariel Sharon,
Israeli Defence Minister

August, 1982

Win some, lose some. Israel appeared to be winning little and losing all. As Beirut crumbled, so did world support. The United States continued to irritate its allies and the Soviets alike by trying to stop the construction of a gas pipeline from Russia to the West. Poland suffered, missiles multiplied, talks failed, strikes crippled, Afghanistan gasped, the Middle East collapsed, Latin America burned. But at least the situation in Africa was only disastrous.

'Of course . . . *NOW* I recognise you!'

WORLD OPINION
P.L.O.
BEIRUT
LURIE
THE TIMES, LONDON

ISRAEL'S IMAGE
BEIRUT
P.L.O.
LURIE
THE TIMES, LONDON

AFRICAN UNITY
AFRICAN SUMMIT
LURIE
THE TIMES, LONDON

LURIE THE TIMES, LONDON
UNI
TY
PLO

Assad of Syria

Felipe Gonzalez, New Leader of Spain

September 1982

If confession is good for the soul, it was a great month fo souls. Yassir Arafat visited the Pope, though any confes sions made in Rome remained necessarily secret Menachem Begin had nothing to confess, since he sav nothing, heard nothing of a massacre in Beirut whic appeared to have taken place under the unwatchful eyes o his troops. Israel was split into two camps: 3,999,99 Israelis on one side, and Mr Menachem Begin on th other. Mexico confessed that it was bankrupt and asked fo suggestions for ways to get out of the mess. The rest of th world confessed that it had no ideas and in any case had perfectly good mess of its own to be getting on with Ronald Reagan triumphantly imposed sanctions agains his European allies in order to punish the Russians fo being beastly to the Poles.

Daniel Arap Moi, President of Kenya

LURIE
THE TIMES, LONDON
LOANS
MEXICO
3m
2m
1m
OIL
REVENUES

"Weinberger? Reagan here — I've got the Russian. Over."

gold
gold
gold
price
gold
gold
gold
LURIE ©
THE TIMES, LONDON

LURIE © THE TIMES, LONDON
GROWING UNEMPLOYMENT
CRIME
RISE

"Wait, Pope — you ain't heard nothin' yet!"

Yasuhiro Nakasone,
candidate for Japan's Premiership

Yuri V. Andropov, new U.S.S.R. boss

October 1982

It was a month of ups and downs. Up went gold prices, up went a Chinese nuclear missile, up went hopes of peace in the Middle East. Down went interest rates, down went Helmut Schmidt, down came hopes of peace in the Middle East. Solidarity resolutely refused to stay down, and began to take on the appearance of a tiger with nine lives. Wall Street decided that things were looking up, and sent share prices booming. In the Lebanon anyone looking up saw only rain pouring on their roofless heads. Israeli political stocks rose as an inquiry into the Beirut massacre looked like getting down to serious business. Prince Andrew of Britain provided some light relief by flying down to Mustique with a porno movie actress Koo Stark. Everyone seemed to know what he was up to, even the British, and morale rose accordingly.

LURIE
THE TIMES, LONDON
E
E
C
W. GERMAN
ECONOMY
INTERNAL
POLITICS

LEBANON
'82
LURIE (with apologies to Picasso's "Guernica")
THE TIMES, LONDON

G. Spadolini, Prime Minister of Italy

"He just keeps on running away, dammit!"

“See? I’m coming down faster than you!”

China develops a submarine-launched nuclear missile

"Let's keep moving . . . otherwise those terrible birds will get us!"

‘Antisemites!’

JA
MAY 0 5 2006
L161—O-1096